RM

Published by Rexi Media

www.reximedia.com

Copyright © 2008 Carmen Taran

ISBN 978-0-615-24520-1

For information about special discounts for bulk purchases,

please contact info@reximedia.com

Production and Marketing Executive: Danielle Daly

Peer Review: Elaine Parrish, Grant Ricketts, Evelyn Lee, Timothy Prentiss, Janis
                  Kelsey, Shri Nandan, James Luyirika-Sewagudde Jr., Luminita
                  Ciumpe, Iris Varga, Charles Hurd, Fengxiang Li.

Design Director: Paul Clothier

This book is dedicated to you.

Table of Contents

why better beginnings

"I married a man for his body." This was the opening of a business presentation I heard a few years ago about the power of decisions. There are a few other beginnings I still remember. One person recently started her sales presentation with "Hi, I am Cheryl, and I am here to save you from yourselves." That got my attention. Another started with a question: "What if you could own the Internet?" A respectable man with a respectable corporate job shocked us with this start: "Like many of the great blues and jazz artists of our time, I found myself onstage at Carnegie Hall high on drugs."

Contrast the examples above with this one that we typically hear when we enter a conference room:

> "Hi everyone, how are you all doing this morning?! I, um… sorry about the projector, can't seem to get it focused, couldn't find the audio-visual guy… does that look readable? There's a handout if you can't… so, anyhow, um, yes, I'm the VP of Marketing at Tedium Inc., started as an account exec and have been with Tedium for about 5 years now, quite a journey I can tell you, it was real different in those days… so, yeah, I want to show you a few slides today—is this mic working? Can you all hear me OK?—on how to market your product effectively, and I'm hoping that… dang, I hate these lapel mics… you might get a few ideas you can use. Are you ready?"

Does this beginning sound familiar?

For the past year I calculated meticulously, and the presenters I heard failed to mention anything noteworthy for the first 13 minutes, on average. In this period, listeners had enough time to think about shopping lists, their next vacation, and all sorts of exciting fantasies.

We've been stuck for too long in lean-back presentations, where participants rely on digital pacifiers for meaningful stimulation. Today, in most business presentations, participants are dripping with digital devices. Between laptops, cell phones, and flash disks, they have instant access to at least a terabyte of data. If we do not capture attention quickly, the listeners' temptation to indulge in digital pleasures is imminent. Unlike before, they can now escape muddy introductions.

This book will teach you how to get participants' spines erect and minds engaged in the first 30 seconds. No more unimaginative, uneasy beginnings. Whether you present face-to-face or virtually, and work in sales or marketing, or train or educate others, or you deliver speeches to inspire, you will benefit from an outstanding beginning. Why? Because we recall beginnings and endings more often than middles. And recall leads to action. If you want to move others toward any action, you have better chances with a strong beginning and a strong ending.

Look at it this way. Science tells us that we can process about 7 bits of information (sound, visual, emotion, or thought) during 1/18 of a second. In an hour, we can process about half a million bits. By the age of 70, if you have been awake for 16 hours a day, you will have processed about 185 billion bits of information. Imagine if out of those billions of bits, people *still* remember the ones you delivered? I am not talking about the Martin Luther King Jr. or Lincoln kind of introductions. I am talking about the kind that you hear at work, in a formal presentation, at a conference, seminar, sales pitch or after-dinner speech. How do you get people to remember those?

A good speaker with bad beginnings

is like a fitness trainer who smokes.

Looking back over the presentations you've heard, how many beginnings do you still remember? Two, three, five at the most? The reason is that they lacked one or more of the techniques described here: anticipation, specificity, inquiry, incongruity, novelty, uncertainty, complexity, ease of comprehension, indulgence and staging. A presenter at an advertising conference recently spoke about the importance of branding and being perceived as #1 in customers' minds. He started this way:

> "What is the tallest mountain in the world? [Audience quickly agrees, more or less accurately, that it's Everest.] What is the second tallest mountain in the world? [Audience: uhhh...] What music band sold the most albums? [Audience quickly agrees it's the Beatles.] What band sold the second highest number of albums? [Audience: uhh…] Do you remember the first person you made love to? [Audience: yes.] Do you remember the second person you made love to? [uhh…] [pause] Do you see the difference between being #1 and #2? In this presentation, I will share three branding techniques you can use to start being recognized as #1."

Notice the techniques included in this example: anticipation, specificity, inquiry, and incongruity. These are the kinds of beginnings that survive the blurry billions of bits that accost us. Some presenters think that if they organize the first sentences well and speak coherently, that's good enough. It isn't. Good intros are the kind that contain insight and announce a profound experience. Good intros have edge and emotion. Good intros make listeners hold their heads still and focus, with widened eyes and parted or pouted lips. In fact, these body cues should be your measurement for delivering great beginnings.

If you were to attend a presentation on weight loss, which introduction would get your attention right away?

> **Example 1.** "We live in times when obesity has reached epidemic proportions, both here in North America, and throughout the industrialized and developing world. There are millions of obese adults worldwide, suffering from problems such as cardiovascular disease, cancer, and diabetes. Nutrition and lifestyle play a critical role at all stages in life, from infancy to old age...." (beginning of a forgettable book).

> **Example 2.** "Okay. Use your head. You need to get healthy if you want to get skinny. Healthy = skinny. Unhealthy = fat. The first thing you need to do is give up your gross vices. Don't act surprised! You cannot expect to eat the same shit and get skinny…" (beginning of bestseller *Skinny Bitch*).

The second example gets attention because it's succinct, specific, easy to understand, and provocative. Even if you replaced the strong words with milder ones, it would get attention. The first example is impersonal, pretentious, and numbs the desire to hear more.

When you fill the first unforgiving 30 seconds with something that has impact, edge, and emotion, you earn the right to be heard.

Can you think of books where the first lines immediately grabbed you? Novelists have long known how to capture attention quickly. Imagine if we started business presentations this way:

"The moment one learns English, complications set in."

Felipe Alfau, Chromos

"The past is a foreign country; they do things differently there."

L. P. Hartley, The Go-Between

"Dr. Weiss, at forty, knew that her life had been ruined by literature."

Anita Brookner, The Debut

We can quickly recognize a good beginning when someone says something extraordinary, something you would like to remember forever so you can tell others. There is an initial spark that you sense will be followed by substance. The question is… how do you say something appealing in the beginning without giving too much away? How do you select just the right words, which would make the listener crave more? What kind of beginning could you create to enchant, fascinate, tantalize, charm, or bewitch your audience?

Read on.

anticipation

Anticipation is like a sixth sense. Just like a lion anticipating the trajectory of its prey, we like to foresee our future state (actions, words, sounds). Hockey players admit that they don't skate toward the puck; they anticipate where the puck is going and skate in that direction. Anticipation often defies the laws of physics: the effect precedes the cause. We laugh before someone is about to tickle us and our digestive system is ready to process food and we salivate before we take the first bite.

Many tasks we set out to complete take place in the mind first (eating, finishing a project, making love). We anticipate the future and map out things we do: walking, working with tools, feeling pleasure or pain, finishing other people's sentences. We interact with the world not only physically but in our minds, and we live through anticipations and mental images. Otherwise, how could we explain that Emily Dickinson wrote such touching, romantic poetry, yet she never had a lover in real life and she hardly even left her house? The mind can be so powerful in anticipation that there are people who read sheet music and enjoy the "sounds," without needing to listen to the symphony.

As Sir Francis Bacon observed hundreds of years ago, anticipation and wonder are the purest form of pleasure. Let's see how you can create anticipation in your speech and give your audience the pleasure of wondering.

How can you paint a picture for your audience in the first 30 seconds? One way is to use words such as "new," "now," "at last," "imagine," and phrases such as "looking forward to" or "can't wait to…" Such phrases create anticipation by generating curiosity and eagerness. Here are a few examples:

"Today we will be *unveiling* four *new features* of our software program."

"*I am looking forward to* showing you what adolescent behavior can teach us about the future of business."

"'For most of us, the day is never done… Why is this? Does it just take too much time to get anything done these days? *At last* [pause], a program that improves your productivity and eliminates the need for overtime."

"*Imagine* what it would be like to disconnect from the brain chatter that connects you to the external world."

"Hans Rosling shows the best stats you've *ever seen*."

"*I've been looking forward to* showing you something that has literally *just come out* of the lab, and which will forever change how we interact with computers."

The cautionary advice with these phrases is that you have to mean them. Years of advertising have numbed us to some of these key words; avoid making fake claims or inflating the trivial. Announcing that you are going to speak about the "new employee care" program right after layoffs does not build credible anticipation.

Anticipation also springs from promising a clear, coherent, well-structured presentation, with pragmatic outcomes: "How can you design, implement, and audit energy-efficient and inexpensive solar power systems for homes and offices? In this presentation, you will hear case studies and see illustrations about new solar technologies, how you can design them…how you can conserve energy, and reduce costs through the use of solar power. At the end of the presentation you will walk away with complete details on environmental design, plus rebate procedures and forms."

Announcing that surprise guests will join the presentation midway or promising rewards for participation build anticipation, because they announce variety and unpredictability.

Even negative words can generate anticipation. Using "not," "don't," "worst," or "only" creates curiosity by providing an unexpected point of view: "I am going to tell you about 100 companies that don't matter in the digital industry." Or "I will share with you reasons to make a not-to-do list." Or "I will share 10 reasons not to use Firefox" (for a playful tone, the purpose would be to get them to use the program and some of the reasons would include "because it's too easy to use" or "it does not crash" or "it does not have any viruses"). Once in a while, consider starting with alternative language that has negative connotations to deviate from the pervasive positivism that reigns over most communication.

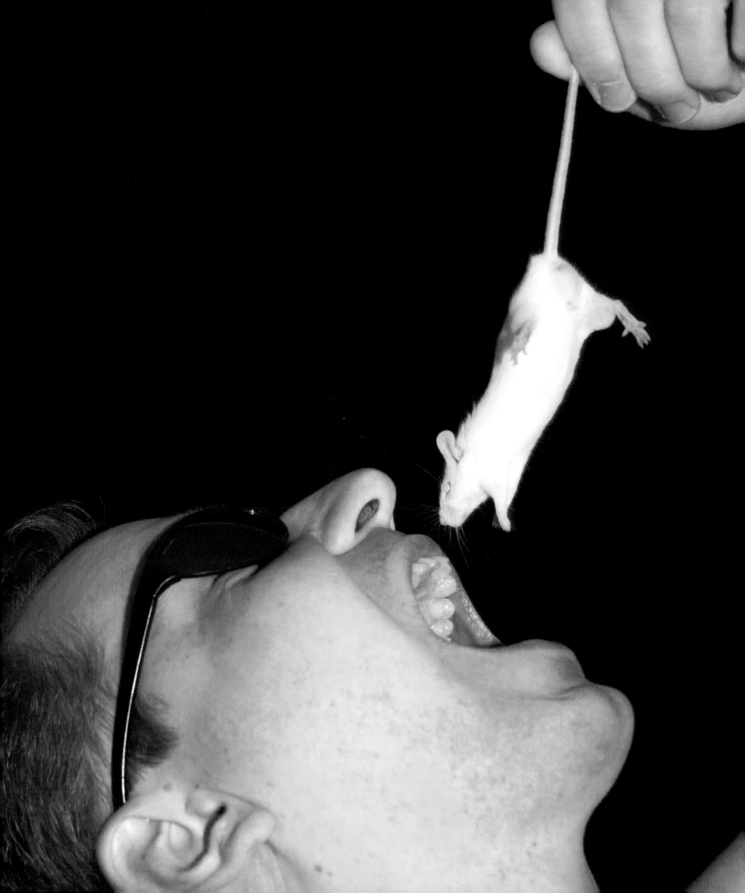

The ability to create anticipation in the first 30 seconds buys you about 10 more minutes of speaking.

After which you have to reapply.

You can generate anticipation even *before* your appearance. Take a look at the title of your speech. Titles such as "Caterpillars and Other Special People" or "What they never told you about…" or "I think therefore iPod" stand out from rigid announcements. Something like "Till Debt Do Us Part" builds more anticipation than "Post-marital financial optimization."

Having someone introduce you in a creative, exciting way builds up your skills and the clout of your session:

> "On August the 25th, out of 25,000 other contestants, from 14 countries, Darren LaCroix was crowned the 2001 World Champion of Public Speaking. Darren is the first person from any New England state to win the championship since the contest began in 1938. As a result of winning, Darren has presented in Malaysia, Taiwan, and Oman. He left his day job of eleven years to pursue a speaking and comedy career full time. As far as late-night comics go—Letterman, Leno, Carson—Darren has listened to them all. (Audience laughter) Please welcome the 2001 World's Speaking Champion, Darren LaCroix."

Best to write your own introduction and ask MCs to deliver it than rely on their impromptu speaking skills. Include in your introduction the title, purpose of the speech, and what qualifies you to give it. Some humor is helpful because you can gauge the audience's emotional level before you appear on the stage. If they don't laugh, bad news—you're going to have to work harder.

specificity

To learn how to be specific, you must get Naked.

Naked is a juice brand that knows how to attract attention with specificity. When you read the information on the Naked Blue Machine, you know that it contains exactly "27 blueberries, 3 blackberries, 3 apples, and 1 banana. […] No added sugar, no preservatives, no inhibitions." This gets more attention than the typical promotions, which advertise a "unique, delicious, refreshing" drink.

Concrete information (e.g., data, anecdotes, biographies, or statistics) attracts attention because specifics mobilize the brain. Does this data capture you?

> "Are you ready to connect with 5 billion people? By 2015, this will be possible. Twenty years ago there were almost no mobile users; today there are almost 3 billion. Low costs are encouraging 10 million users to join the communication party every month…" (Mika Vehvilainen, Nokia Siemens Networks).

> "Ninety-four percent of job applicants do not get a call back – ever." (John Younger, Accolo).

> "7.6 billion years from now, the sun will reach its maximum size as a red giant: its surface will extend beyond the Earth's orbit today by 20% and will shine 3,000 times brighter. In its final stage, the sun will collapse into a white dwarf." (David Appell, *Scientific American*).

When you use specific details, make them fact-packed, telegraphic, with very few adjectives. No redundant, needless words. No fat.

Certain informal discussions took place involving a full and frank exchange of views out of which there arose a series of proposals which, on examination proved to indicate certain promising lines of enquiry, which, when pursued led to the realization that the alternative courses of action might, in fact, in certain circumstances, be susceptible to discrete modification leading to a reappraisal of the original areas of difference and pointing the way to encouraging possibilities of compromise and cooperation, which, if bilaterally implemented with appropriate give and take on both sides might, if the climate were right, have a reasonable possibility at the end of the day, of leading rightly or wrongly to a mutually satisfactory resolution.

The paragraph to the left, extracted from the British comedy series *Yes Prime Minister*, could easily be part of the introduction to a modern business speech. Imagine that instead of all the contorted, generic phrases, you would simply say "We could do a deal."

Specific, concrete, down-to-earth information provides credibility by anchoring the content into reality much better. Specificity also sets the message apart from hundreds of other messages that start the same way. Unfortunately, too many speakers deliver content in a Pavlovian manner, programmed by years of corporate schooling or popular generic language.

As a culture, we have become too used to generic words. We describe things as great, interesting, mind-boggling, amazing, awesome, whatever. When unusual weather is approaching, we say the sky is "weird." Compare that to: "The sky above the port was the color of television, tuned to a dead channel." (William Gibson, *Neuromancer)*.

Corporate clichés are often the culprit for generic beginnings. We've heard so often those cautious phrases, sandwiched by greasy language that talks about paradigm shifts, synergies, and holistic approaches…words that make us about as excited as a cow on its way to the opera. Why parrot lazy, generic language when we live life in non-generic terms? Why not challenge ourselves to draw fresh terms from the three-quarters of a million words available in the English language?

William Horton, design specialist, makes the following remarks regarding the rhetoric of various documents:

> Gettysburg Address: 266 words
>
> Ten Commandments: 297 words
>
> Box of cereal: 1,200 words
>
> U.S. Government order on pricing cabbage: 26,911 words

It's not the number of words that you use, but rather their special fabric. The reason we pay so much for food at restaurants is because menu creators know how to use specific language that stimulates the senses. You're not just buying a bunch of veggies and fish, you're buying "delicate, herbaceous halibut served on a bed of forbidden rice, with aphrodisiac dhal, freshened with a cucumber dill salad"; and you're not just buying chocolate dessert, you're buying "a sinful combination of bourbon-soaked vanilla beans and fresh raspberries with a chocolate ganache surprise." Salivating?

By comparison, using corporate clichés or painfully generic language puts people off immediately. The greatest lesson I learned from a literature professor related to specificity is this: "If they cannot repeat it, they didn't get it. And if they didn't get it, why would they want to contribute to your cause?"

Be careful of seductive details. If the information is specific but not related to the content, the listener may remember the interesting details and not the important information. How many commercials have you seen where you remember the beautiful blonde but forget whether she had a bottle of beer or a bottle of mouthwash in her hand? Peripherals may heighten interest but may detract from what's important.

Any ordinary word used with fresh applications that can create a sensory experience will catch attention more than faded language. Starving the adjectives and feeding the verbs helps you to add energy to your words and makes an introduction punchier:

"The company is hemorrhaging money."

"We scissored the competition."

"We cratered the deal."

To embed more vivid sentences and colorful rhetoric into your introductions, consider these steps.

Read any printed materials. The spoken word is always hurried, but the written one offers commitment.

Listen to how others speak, what kind of words work for them. What causes ennui? What words raise your eyebrows?

Take notes, review them often, and practice. Practice saying them. Yes, even the gods practice.

How do you know whether the language that you're using is specific and has good rhetoric? "It's like dating," writer Amy Krouse Rosenthal says. "Some sentences, no matter how well-dressed or nice, just don't do it for me. Others I click with instantly. It could be something as simple yet weirdly potent as a single word choice (tangerine). We're meant to be, that sentence and me. And when it happens, you just know." What sentences could you include in your first 30 seconds that your audience would want to date?

In the beginning of a speech, view specifics and rhetoric as survival. Nothing puts an audience off more than uncommitted, detached, milky phrases. The rhetoric of the introduction announces the quality of the rest of the speech.

Notice the difference between these two introductions:

Example 1. "American culture is experiencing a downturn. The population is paying exorbitant prices for water goods and feel uncomfortable about the existing situation. People are subjected to extended commutes on a daily basis and are unhappy about fuel costs. People are exposed to media celebrities engaged in unethical acts and yet feel culpable for watching them on television. People also become considerably upset at individuals who do not have cellular phone manners in public, despite the fact that everybody engages in frequent use of text messaging devices."

Example 2. "There's something rotten in the state of America. It is something phony, belligerent, and toxic in the culture. We pay two dollars a bottle for water and feel like suckers. We commute ninety minutes a day in our SUVs and complain about gas prices. We watch Paris Hilton on *Larry King Live* the day after she gets out of jail for drunk driving and feel like dopes for watching. We get furious at the loud cell-phone talker in the waiting room as we bang out e-mails on BlackBerries with our angry thumbs..." (Dick Meyer, *Why We Hate Us*).

Always be authentic and specific in the way you speak. Stop achieving "synergy" by using a "holistic approach." Don't worry about "leveling the playing field" or "leveraging your talent." If you "have a lot on your plate," it'd better be a large slice of pizza. And if you want to "interface" with someone or "touch bases," do it the literal way and not on company property.

inquiry

Asking questions sends the message that you're treating each participant as more than a mere fixture in the audience. It also implies immediate participation because every time you ask a question, the listener's brain is mandated to answer:

"Are computers the masters and users the servants?"

"Should you ever respond to spam?"

"Why is it so hard to swat a fly?"

"What will the corporation of the future look like?"

Did you attempt to answer the questions when you read them? If the questions had been the introduction to a presentation, would you have been intrigued right away? The more provocative the question, the more immediate the involvement and promising the beginning.

"Can women and men be friends?"

"Are your eyeballs the size at birth that they will be your whole life?"

"What would computers be like if we had no hands?"

Consider asking questions to introduce a contradiction or some disturbing information or play the devil's advocate to stimulate the listeners.

"What exactly is that 'new car' smell?"

"Can you predict human behavior?"

"What do schoolteachers and sumo wrestlers have in common?"

If you want immediate attention,
ask a question.

Useful categories of questions are the "have you ever…", "if…", or "imagine…" types. The more down-to-earth and realistic, the faster the rapport with the audience:

"Have you ever considered plastic surgery?"

"If you wanted to make a difference in someone's life every day, how would you do it?"

"If you could modify one piece of our software, what would it be?"

"Imagine you're 35,000 feet up, a few hours into a cross-country airplane journey. Having worked on some office memos, you finally get around to watching the DVD of *Murder on the Orient Express* on your laptop. But just as Detective Poirot is revealing whodunit, the screen goes blank. Your laptop's batteries have run out of juice. What to do?" (Stephen Cass, *Discover*)

When you ask questions, make sure they are related to the content.

"Did you know that the dog who played the female collie Lassie was in fact male? Wild, huh? Today, we will look at the impact of the economy on…"

When you ask a question, pause to give participants time to answer (even if it's a silent answer). Too many speakers ask a question and immediately move on to the next idea. Be prepared to follow a question with another as you watch people's bodies and hear their voices when they answer. Sometimes, we get too attached to a script and forget to build off what the audience gives us. The detour may be worthwhile.

The phrasing and complexity of the questions will impact the response time and depend on your audience's background knowledge. If you have all day, and are surrounded by super experts, you can ask a deep question: "If quantum physics is the clearer picture of how the universe really is, and everything is merely a perception, how do we know that we're really alive?" If not, asking "Do you think we all see things differently?" will get the conversation going faster.

For additional inquiry methods, Google *Socratic questioning* (clarification questions; probing assumptions, rationale, or evidence; questioning viewpoints, perspectives, implications, and consequences); you will have access to an even wider inventory of question types.

As you ask questions, create a space in your mind, between your thoughts, where you can "place" the answers you receive. It's often difficult to quiet your thoughts to receive input, but it is so rewarding because the participant notices you paid attention and did not judge. Accepting answers with a "quiet" mind is like temporary meditation (read more about this in the *Tranquility* section, on page 183).

incongruity

Incongruity is a conflict between what participants expect to see or hear and what actually occurs. An introduction such as "I hate housework. You make the bed, you do the dishes, and six months later you have to start all over again" guides listeners down one cognitive path and derails them at the end.

Typically, the more unexpected the event, the greater the cognitive arousal. Looking at the picture on the left, participants would find themselves intrigued by the contrast. For instance, the graphic could be the introductory message to a presentation that discusses bringing in the new while respecting the old in a specific business area.

Remember the introduction quoted in the beginning: "Like many of the great blues and jazz artists of our time, I found myself onstage at Carnegie Hall high on drugs"? The speaker, an avid trombone player, explained how he went to Carnegie Hall to perform, and broke his wrist 24 hours before the concert. He went to the hospital, had a cast put on, was pumped full of drugs to relieve the pain, and went on stage as planned.... Onstage, at Carnegie Hall, high on drugs…" In a similar way, a corporate executive started with "When I was in prison… [pause] visiting…" Imagine the audience after these kinds of beginnings. Pulling the rug out from underneath us with incongruity causes increased curiosity and attention.

You can create incongruity with startling information or blunt beginnings. "Lie detectors lie," writes Jonathan Kwitney, in the beginning of his book *The Dirty Little Secret of Lie Detectors*, an introduction that surprises and entices further attention. Or "The U.S. Department of Labor estimates that today's learner will have 10–14 jobs by the age of 38."

Incongruous information provides opportunities for reflection. For instance, disturbing information such as the number of deaths caused by smoking, or rising unemployment rates, or world starvation, leads to increased attention. Providing listeners with the opportunity to ask "How come?" is a strong technique to ensure that they are paying attention.

Incongruity is based on surprise and surprise predicts interest… but only when the surprise is reduced and there is resolution: "Did you know that the human brain is still smarter than the latest, super-sophisticated computer? [pause] Here is how electronic networks operate and how the brain operates…." Or… "Want a sharper memory and a more agile mind? The solution might be just one video game away."

The impact of incongruity depends on a person's background knowledge. The more a person knows, the more likely that conflict will occur because there is a lot of material to conflict against. If someone is new to Freud, a topic in *Freud: From Jewish to Atheism* would not create that much conflict.

Conflict in the first sentence alone is not sufficient. If the first statement poses a conflict, the next one should resolve it and pose at least one more. Just as the old British anecdote has it:

> They only got one bar! Boooo!
>
> But it's 20 feet long! Hurrah!
>
> They don't sell any beer! Boooo!
>
> They're giving it all away! Hurrah!
>
> They don't have any barmen! Boooo!
>
> Just barmaids! Hurrah!

Notice the conflict-resolution-conflict sequencing in an introduction for a business presentation:

> "Let's pull off the Band-Aid quickly. You've come to believe that mutual funds are a smart place to put your money. They are not. That's the assessment of the smartest minds in finance, supported by a mountain of historical data. If you own managed mutual funds, you will almost certainly retire with less money—a lot less money—than if you had simply dumped your money into boring index funds. So two questions: how can this be true? And why, in gleeful defiance of data, do more people keep buying mutual funds every year?" (Dan Heath and Chip Heath, *Fast Company*).

It is this constant sequencing of conflicts and resolutions that keeps people paying attention and it is what keeps us reading mystery novels at 3 am.

You can create incongruity with ambivalence, which provides the coexistence of two conflicting issues, such as attitude toward food or love/hate in relationships: "Listen to what I'm telling you, damn it, 'cause I brought you into this world, and I can take you out of it." (Bill Cosby). In a business presentation, you can include ambivalence by mentioning love/hate relationships between HR and IT, customers and service reps, or employees and managers:

"Who is the most important person in your office?" [Audience likely to respond: the boss.] Yes, the boss is the most important person. Why is that? [Wait for audience responses; some answers mention how bosses impact raises and judge performance.] Yes, these are valid reasons. But here is another very important one: they impact our well-being. Because the boss can make the blood boil. In fact, recent surveys show that they can even increase our risk for heart disease… What can we do about this?..." (Willow Lawson, adapted from *Psychology Today*).

Any time you present a new reality, participants try to fit it within their existing view of the world. It is this quest that keeps them paying attention and wondering what will come next. At the opposite spectrum of incongruity is the inclusion of truisms in opening statements. Any self-evident truth (e.g., "To survive in business one must be competitive" or "A sales pitch should outline the benefits of the product") is not an attention-grabber.

We persist in activities that have enough conflict to keep us interested.
Interest fades when there is no conflict.

novelty

Novelty creates interest because new events often compete with existing expectations. If you've been using the same software for a year, a new upgrade gets your attention. If you've been used to square tea bags, a round tea bag surprises you. In a town with old cars, a new one will catch your eye. Imagine when you hear a speech that starts by disclosing something new:

> "In my vault I have cells that reverse paralysis in sheep that have spina bifida and can't walk. After we injected our cells, the first animal treated returned to normal and was walking fine. The same model could work for paralyzed humans." (Robert Lanza, *Discover*)

Presenting something new and *creating* something new are different things. Presenting novelty is obviously easier. All you have to do is stay tuned to world news, politics, arts, and popular entertainment gossip, talk to your R&D department about recent innovations in your field or company…and have a good memory. To raise eyebrows and get the parted lips, consider generating your own novelty, or at a minimum, *proposing* novel changes to accustomed ways of doing things.

Creating something entirely new is difficult (almost everything is rooted in something else). However, the exercise is worthwhile not only to receive immediate attention but to get you prepared for future professions. Do not be surprised if in the future, a popular job title will be **Imagination Therapist**, a person who can free us from painfully linear and restrictive thinking. An imagination therapist would convince us to stretch our creativity and, using elements from Jungian therapy and yoga, would help us become more emancipated. Would you like this job?

To create novelty, do this quick test: Fold your hands by interlocking all your fingers. Which thumb falls on top? The right one or left? Now interlock all your fingers again forcing the other thumb to be on top. Do the same test by crossing your arms naturally, then reverse them. If it feels uncomfortable, you're doing it right. That's what novelty and creativity sometimes entail.

A creative way to generate novelty is to find new uses for old ideas. Passing by a junkyard, the average person will see a pile of metal fossils, randomly thrown around. The novelty-seeking person will see shape, and texture, and lines, and colors that have escaped the untrained eye. They will see the beauty in the old, which can be morphed into something new. Let that person be you.

When the British department store Marks & Spencer (M&S) became involved in the sandwich business, they found a major inefficiency: English people like their sandwiches with butter, which meant that employees had to put it on bread by hand. This hindered scalability. When a manager visited a home section of the M&S store, he noticed how sheets were made by using a silkscreen process to print patterns. He replaced the ink with butter and provided a solution for scaling the process of bread buttering. Can you think of any fields outside of your business that resemble the processes and products you offer? Can you use an existing element with a new intention? Imagine a presentation that started this way: "While our existing drug, Minoxidil, did not prove successful for treating high blood pressure, we've been following up on one of its side effects: hair growth. With a few additional touches, we can release a new drug. I'm thinking of calling it Rogaine."

You can also generate novelty by combining existing ideas. The creation of Sun Microsystems' Java language is a perfect example. The developers did not ultimately generate anything new; they borrowed from existing software constructs, similar to C++, Smalltalk, and Lisp. Are there any elements in your existing business that you could combine to generate something new? Imagine your audience's reaction when you start by presenting your "new" discovery.

One of the greatest examples of modifying an existing concept is the creation of the famous lemon squeezer by Philippe Starck, who got inspired by observing a lemon being squeezed over a squid. The designer claims that his object is not meant to squeeze lemons but rather start conversations. What can you create that would start a conversation?

You can introduce your topic in a new light by simply changing the **order** in which everyone is used to seeing it. Imagine if you started your presentation this way:

"Let's look at this diagram that you have seen for the past two years. What if we were to rotate it by 45°?"

"What if we were to decrease the amount of cream and replace it with …air?" (they actually do that in some ice creams)

"What if we were to eliminate two steps from our process?"

"What if we were to reverse steps 3 and 4?"

"What if we increased the frequency of our distribution?"

"What if we take this apart and reassemble it this way?"

"What if we add vanilla flavor to it?"

Anytime you change something related to the growth or evolution of your product or service, you have the possibility to generate something new. Since perceiving order is one of the most simple and fundamental experiences that humans recognize (one of our first sensations as humans is the order of the mother's heartbeats when we are in the womb), it will be easy to appeal quickly to an audience by presenting changed order, therefore novelty.

Imagine if you started your presentation by proposing to alter the **structure** of your products or services. Structure is what makes an object intelligible to the world. Look at any object that is part of your business and wonder: What is it similar to, what are its dimensions, how does it impact the senses, what distinguishes it from something else? Presentations that start by introducing novel ideas for exciting restructuring of routine parts, shapes, or behaviors get immediate attention:

"Our customers have been used to square tea bags. What if we made them round. Or triangular? Or pyramidal?"

"Our customers have been used to black or silver laptops. What if they could get them in any color? What if we offered them in pink?"

"Our students would love to combine different modules from different courses into one page. What if we created a portal that allowed them to do just that?"

Even the ubiquitous "re-org" in a corporation gets immediate attention when presented, especially if it's a wise one, not just a seasonal habit. When a scientist was researching DNA sequencing, for instance, he got inspired from an earlier interest in Gothic architecture, which he used as a source of inspiration for DNA molecular structure. Imagine the beginning of his speech when he presented his ideas. The more you think about distinctions and contrasts about your offerings, the more innovative your work style, the hotter your skills, and consequently, the better your beginnings when you speak about your ideas or creations.

Changing relations (connections or affiliations) adds novelty to your topic. Ask these kinds of questions about your offerings:

"What if we were to reverse it (turn it upside down or inside out)?"

"Can it serve multiple purposes?"

"Could we rearrange all of it, or part of it?"

"Can it be modified? Can parts of it be substituted?"

Here are some examples of beginnings of business presentations, applied to products or services, using the changed relations model:

"Our business is about conference travel. Since travel has become almost an insult for our clients lately, what if we rearranged our model and focused on satellite and Web broadcasting?"

"What if we were to learn from adolescents about the Enterprise of the Future?"

"Could we manufacture our clothes in a more flexible way if we borrowed ideas from spacesuit design?"

You can generate novelty by **changing points of view**. As author Gerard Nierenberg reminds us, the riddle about the king who offered his daughter's hand in marriage is a good example of changing points of view. A king invited three promising knights, put them in a room with no mirrors or reflective surfaces, and told them: "I will place on your forehead either a white or a black dot. If you see two white dots, you can raise your hand. Otherwise, you cannot speak to each other. Whoever comes out of the room and guesses the color of their dot, wins my daughter's hand." Then he placed black dots on all three foreheads. One of the suitors came out of the room and said he had a black dot. How did he know?

The answer rests on the knight's ability to adopt different points of view. The lucky suitor noticed the two black dots on the other two foreheads. He thought: "If the person to my right saw a white dot on me and the black dot we saw in common, then he would figure that he has a black dot and he would storm out of the room. Since he is not saying anything, he must be looking at two black dots, which means I have a black dot."

That's the power of adopting a point of view hypothetically. If you've looked at your business from your eyes only, see what happens when you look at it from the lenses of a business partner, customer, or supplier. Maybe a Martian? Or, more seriously speaking, someone who doesn't even know they want to be your customer or someone who likes to complain all the time or challenges everything.

Changing points of view means adding novelty to your presentation. Eddie Izzard gets attention and laughs with his stand-up comedy when he adopts different points of view. He speaks as a bird ordering white wine in first class, dirt particles that rebel against the vacuum cleaner, and socks that apologize to the pants in the washer for being late.

The more outrageous your ideas, the better for your creative power (you don't have to use audacious ideas, but keep practicing to create them; one in 100 may actually have appeal). Here are some examples of audacious business propositions; imagine the listeners' eyes when the presenter started this way:

"Have you ever noticed how your pets react after you've left them at the kennel for a week while you were sipping cocktails in the tropics? [Pause for people to agree.] Here is our solution for avoiding pet separation anxiety: Pet Music. By listening to our 3-CD set pack, pets will become calmer and owners can save on furniture."

"What if loved ones could send us emails *after* they pass away? [Pause to enjoy them gasping.] Our company, finalthoughts.com, would enable us to write email notes, which will be saved and sent to loved ones after we die."

Keep in mind that novelty is not something new until it is "perceived" as new. Artist Marcel Duchamp created the famous Fountain, which is essentially a urinal. His "masterpiece" was declared an art landmark of the 20th century, and is often considered more important than pieces by Picasso and Matisse. The curious fact is that the object was not deemed newsworthy until others cast judgment and considered it novel. So if novelty is part of your introduction, make sure that the group is likely to view your topic and approach as innovative. Public *recognition* of novelty is as important as novelty *creation*.

To get inspired about generating novelty for your audience, learn from advertising, art, science, haute couture, and R&D departments.

uncertainty

Is anybody out there?

A significant chunk of the universe is missing. 96% to be exact. And no one has a clue what dark matter really is, or why living organisms die, or whether there are better ways to reproduce, or what the stock market will offer tomorrow. But that's OK because we love to investigate and speculate and write research papers and watch horse races and exchange stocks and stay curious.

Uncertainty turns us on.

Isaac Asimov, scientist and fiction writer, used to say that the most exciting phrase to hear in science is not "Eureka" but "That's funny." Knowing that something is true or false is a temporary pleasure. The longer-lasting pleasure comes from "terra incognita," as Daniel Boorstin calls it in *The Discoverers* – unknown territory. TV newscasters know how to capture attention right away (sometimes to the point of frustration) by creating anticipation and uncertainty: "What do experts predict for the stock market in the next few months? What kind of traffic should you expect as the holidays are approaching? All of this and more when we return at 11." People think in trends and while they don't like predictability, they love the quest of predicting.

Not all uncertainty piques our interest. We don't care too much to wait for a doctor's diagnosis or whether it's going to rain tomorrow, knowing we scheduled a picnic. Uncertainty generates interest only when it is an exciting play on alternatives, and it creates pleasant suspense and a fulfilling sense of discovery.

The kind of uncertainty that excites us appears in situations where any number of alternative events can occur, their sequence is unknown, and each event can happen with equal probability. For instance, elections are more interesting when there are four candidates, not two, and when all of them have equal chances. The 2008 men's final at Wimbledon was interesting because it was uncertain who would win. Nadal had as much chance as Federer.

How can you create the thrill of uncertainty in the beginning of a speech? Present the audience with an issue that needs resolving and give them the thrill of "figuring it out." For instance:

> "To create only one version of the customer satisfaction form, we have combined all existing 13 forms and place them in a wiki. During this session, you will log into the wiki and make real-time changes. At the end, we will have only one document and everyone will have contributed and watched everyone else's input. I don't know what the final form will look like yet, but you are in control and I cannot wait to see the result."

> "To improve the quality of our product's Web interface, it is apparent from your past responses that we need a new Web design software. We have six to choose from, provided by different vendors. By the end of this session, you will have a chance to complete three tasks in all six applications and recommend one for the whole department."

That which is uncertain, unpredictable, but solvable will get immediate attention.

The conditions for exciting uncertainty (lots of alternatives, unpredictable occurrence of the solution, equal chances of an alternative to be the solution) resemble the conditions of a game. Consider delivering a presentation in a game format. Why? Imagine listeners looking bored, dissatisfied, heads propped in their hands to prevent them from falling in the event of dozing off. Now imagine placing a game of *Solitaire* in front of them… would you immediately see them change posture, straighten their backs, and even break a smile? Games have the ability to alter our sense of self and time; they awaken curiosity and, most importantly, allow us to be in control.

And boy, do we like to be in control. We think we have systems for predicting where the roulette wheel is going to stop; we think that if we blow on the dice, there is a greater chance of winning. And we think we are luckier if we pick our own lottery numbers. This innate trait is what enables us to get a thrill out of uncertainty.

If you use the "presentation-like game" approach, the beginning needs to include a specific goal ("We will determine how to best create the front Web page of our business"), rules that clarify how the game will take place ("We will work in teams of five, using content provided to each of you"), and directions ("You will have 40 minutes to complete, then each team designates a volunteer to showcase the team's idea, and everyone will vote for the best approach"). The rest of the details can come after the brief introduction. Wanna play?

Using a "presentation-like game" approach secures attention because suddenly, the context is not about the presenter, it is about the participants. Due to the fact that no one knows the outcome (unpredictable) but there will be an outcome (control over the future), people feel appreciated, involved, and focused. An important ingredient in including uncertainty in the beginning of the presentation is to match the challenge presented with the level of participants' skills. The lower the skills, the lower the challenge should be.

Equally important is to vary the difficulty of the game-like approach. If you divide people into groups, or conduct trivia-like games to generate anticipation about the topic, start from easy to difficult, as listeners' skills adjust to the situation: "Together we will find ways to cut our response time to emergency calls by 30%; each team competition will get increasingly difficult. Are you ready?"

For added interest, include hidden information as part of the challenge. In popular games, it is more challenging when you do not know the size of the other team's fleet of ships or where it is hidden. Hypothesizing adds entertainment. If you can include a randomness factor, the arousal is greater (e.g., "In parts of the game, your team will be asked to draw from a deck of cards, which will offer additional challenges"). Announcing a reward for the game, but not disclosing what it is, contributes to the level of excitement and anticipation. Overall, if you have a clear goal, challenges that require some skills (not only chance), and relevant feedback, people will anticipate the thrill of uncertainty.

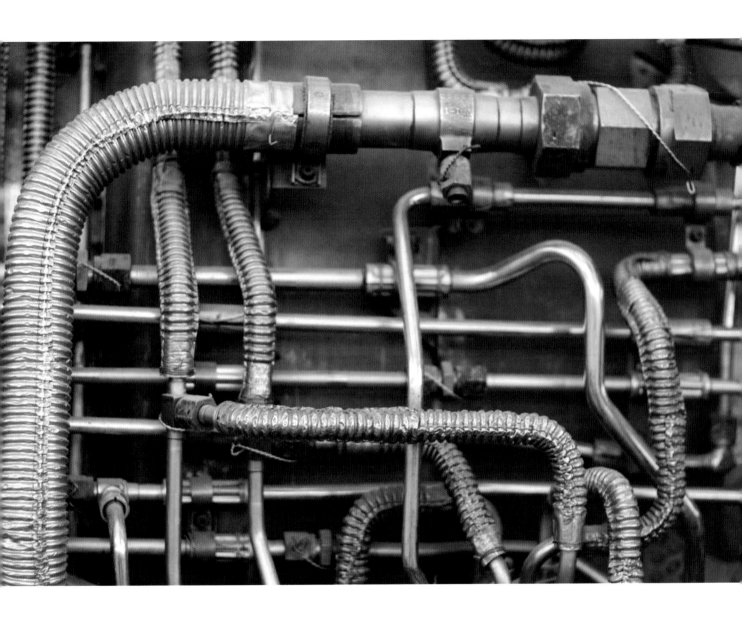

complexity

Complexity generates interest because, unlike simplicity, where the parts predict the whole, in complex patterns, the parts are unpredictable.

Which would hold your interest longer? This picture? Or…

This picture?

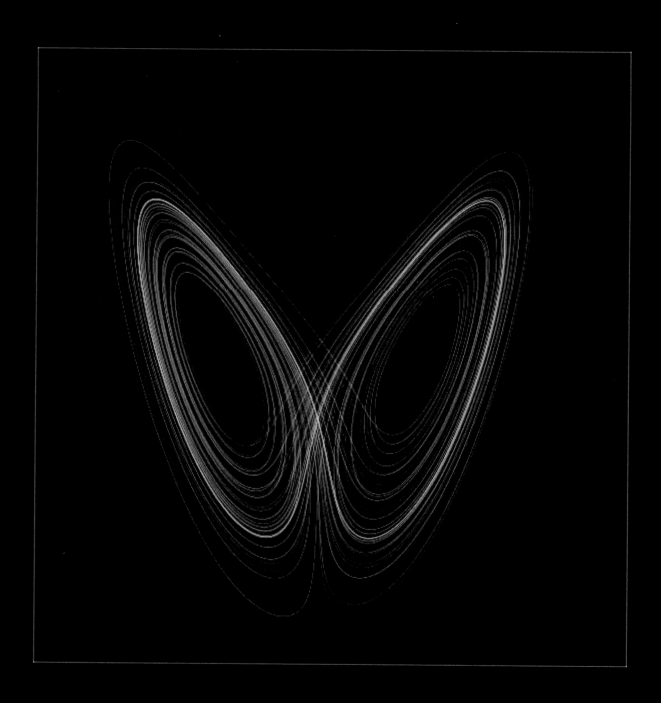

No emotion or event happens in isolation. There is always a link, a connection to something else, a larger context. Ever since *Gilgamesh,* where the hero ponders the human condition in the first known work of literature, 35 centuries ago, we've been accustomed to acknowledging chaos and realizing that we must first recognize the issues in a system before dealing with improvements. The same with Dante's *Divine Comedy*, where the gates of Hell precede the ability to contemplate any solutions for life improvements. As famous psychologist Mihaly Csikszentmihali reminds us, it makes good sense psychologically to admit that ours is a chaotic, complex world.

Most business processes are characterized by disorganization, turbulence, and volatility; just like a tornado, businesses do not progress in a straight line and your audience knows it. Few presenters dare mention it. Acknowledging the complexity of your business, while providing hope for order, establishes the credibility of the speaker and gets attention because of the contrast: is there order in chaos? Yes. Back in 1963, Edward Lorenz, trying to predict weather patterns, generated a visual of a chaotic system over time and noted its "butterfly" shape. Known as the Lorenz Attractor (see graph to the left), it shows for the first time that there is structure underneath an unstructured system. The situation can be the same for your business.

Descartes considered that we can deal with complex problems by dividing them into smaller units that are easier to explain. However, this Cartesian reductionism ignores the relationships between parts and their meaning. The focus is too much on the small parts. Better to acknowledge complexity and treat it as a whole.

As scientists remind us, any system that is ordered will become disordered in time. (Does your desk offer proof?) Even though our businesses are nonlinear and dynamic, there is order underneath the disorder. The order is based on a self-organizing structure or pattern, created by the active relationships that make up the system (e.g., people sometimes organize themselves into crowds without the help of an "invisible hand").

For any presenter who has the courage to discuss solutions for complex issues (e.g., traffic problems, shopping habits, Internet troubles, financial market crashes, cancer, business processes), attention is guaranteed. Why? Because the audience is aware of complexity and becomes curious. In addition, complexity creates a bit of tension, which, when positively induced, can increase interest and attention.

Which introduction would attract your attention more: "There are two reasons why people shop…" or "We have discovered a mechanism to predict shopping habits…"? The first one, while simple, offers passing interest and may be received with skepticism. The second one makes you wonder and anticipate. It also draws attention because people think "Well, if this presenter could predict this complex issue, maybe I can use the same process for my own complex problems." This actually happened. Scientists at Oxford University got inspired by solving complex problems in biology (e.g., nutrient supply-lines in fungus) and are now wondering whether they can apply the same lessons for supply-chain design in retail.

The banking industry is always faced with new challenges such as online procedures, security, regulations, and a rough economy. The advertising industry is also faced with complex challenges: online ads and tracking, behavioral targeting, and respect for privacy. In the shipping industry, a major change occurred with containerization, which dictated the redesign of ships, refrigeration technology, and even port designs. In fact, the ports that adapted are still in business, but the ones that didn't are now shopping malls, entertainment areas, or waterfront apartments, as Grove mentions in *Only the Paranoid Survive*.

The businesses that acknowledge complexity and find the order underneath the disorder are able to stay successful.

To create curiosity with complexity, answer these questions about your business: What elements make it dynamic and what are its unique characteristics? What type of relationships hold the entire system together beneath the apparent disorder? What elements generate instability? What enables it to adapt? What typically arises in the absence of an "invisible hand"?

Always ask the question: What is beneath the surface? Include the answers in your introduction.

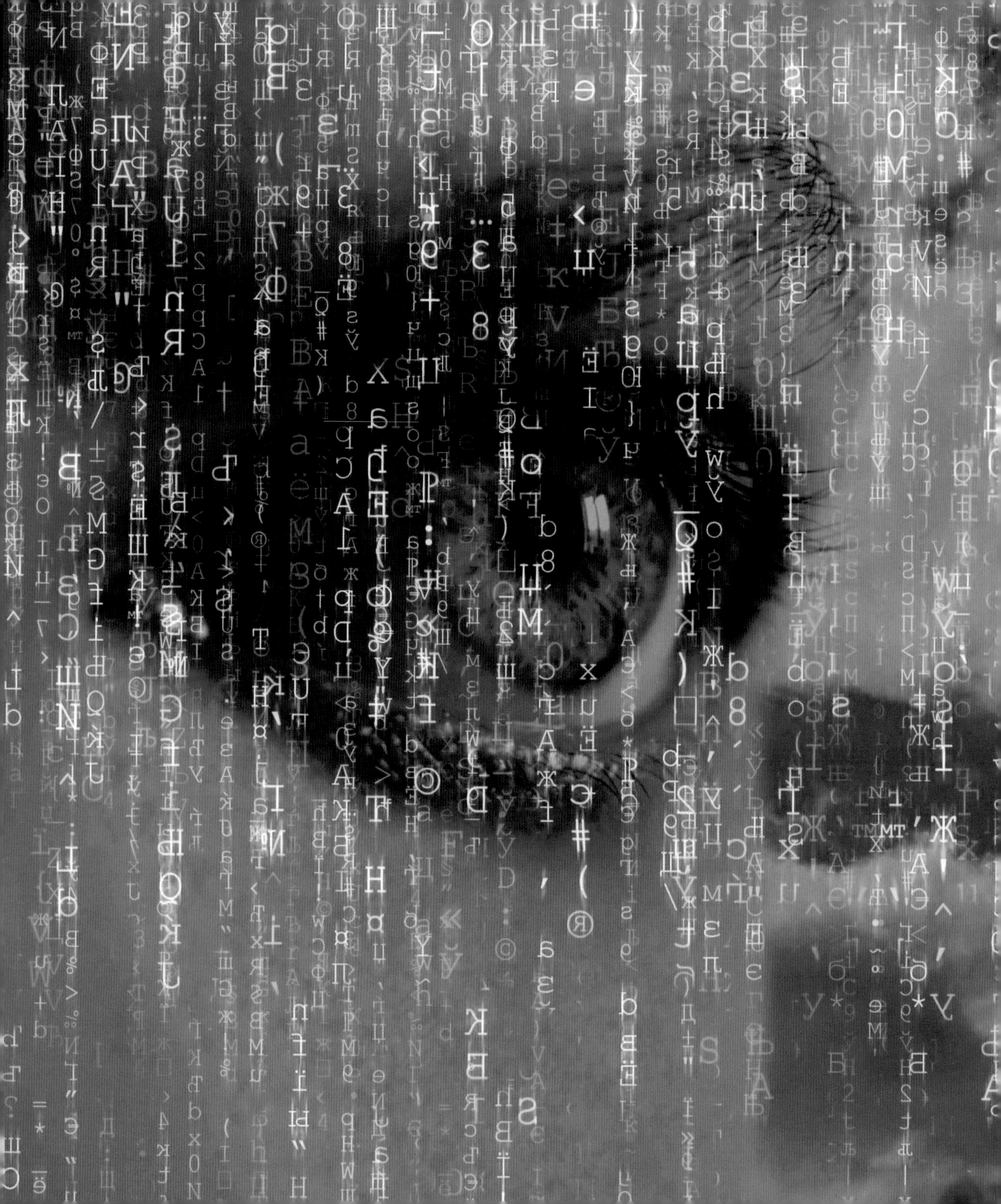

Here is an example of a beginning that acknowledges the complexity of a field and promises the listener some order.

"Some designers believe that successful software development is the result of programming 0s and 1s and arranging pixels in an appealing interface. However, in real life, there is more to software development than crafting well-designed interactions and interfaces. There are timelines that will startle you as they swoosh by and there are budgets that don't go very far or come very near. There are people you work with, who often have different tempers, agendas, emotions, and the right to be wrong. There are technical tools you use that often do not work. [Pause to allow acknowledgement.]

What does it take to create a successful software? I will show you how to calm the chaos and create a **process** that enables you to:

- Finish on **time**

- At the **cost** you had in mind

- With good **quality**

- And using your assigned **resources**."

[Emphasis on the bold words because you know their concerns.]

Notice the unpretentious, down-to-earth language, the warm rhetoric, the inquiry, the anticipation, and the promise to calm down complexity. Anytime you admit that we are surrounded by complex systems but provide participants with hope for order, you have their attention (and you are a hero). When you combine elements of novelty, uncertainty, and complexity (like computer or cell phone manufacturers do), you can have their attention not only for 30 seconds, but for at least 30 days.

ease of comprehension

If you use complexity to attract attention, unlock it somehow to make it penetrable. Ease of comprehension relies on clarity and coherence. How do you achieve this? In addition to the examples provided in the *Specificity* section, use the power of **analogies**. Imagine when presenters start this way:

- "A good strategy makes any tactic work better. A good strategy puts less pressure on executing your tactics perfectly. Let's compare this with skiing. Carving your turns better is a tactic. Choosing the right ski area in the first place is a strategy. Everyone skis better in Utah, it turns out."

- "The universe is expanding. [pause] To understand this, imagine that galaxies are like paper dots stuck onto a balloon; blow it up and the dots don't grow, but they do move apart." (Robert Hubble, scientist).

- " …imagine standing inside a blueberry muffin and looking around. The blueberries surround you left, right, up, and down; whichever way you look, there is no appreciable difference in how they are distributed throughout the muffin. Our view from inside the universe appears to be the same." (Michael Brooks, explaining dark energy).

Effective **comparisons** also lead to ease of comprehension. The famous Pepsi vs. Coke tests, or ads comparing cars or cell phone services attest to the power of comparison. Can you think of an area where you can compare your products or services to similar ones (before/after, old/new, fast/slow) and start a presentation that way? As long as you do not use any derogatory, deceptive, or confusing remarks for your competition, comparisons will help you move an audience to another emotional and intellectual state that is easy to understand and favors your cause.

Poorly structured information wrecks comprehension. To deliver coherent content in the beginning and throughout your speech, categorize it in some way. While information is infinite, the ways of presenting it are not. Whether you divide it chronologically, by category, hierarchy, or by problem-solution, pick an architecture that best suits your audience. Notice in this example the combination of inquiry, specific information, and anticipation of a well-structured speech:

"Did you know that 40 to 50 percent of new hires turn out to be poor performers? It gets worse: 1 top performer equals 3 average performers. How do you solve this problem? In today's presentation, I will share the three most important qualities of top performers: *drive, curiosity, and ethics.* Let's discuss them one at a time…" (John Younger, CEO, Accolo).

"Imagine that you can use your mouse's wheel to whiz past planets, stars, galaxies, dwarfs, black holes, and into deep space. Now you can, either with Google Sky or Microsoft's World Wide Telescope. Let's look at four differences between these two applications and help you decide which application you may want to use." (Robert Scoble, *Fast Company*).

Categorizing information using mnemonic devices, such as acronyms or numbers of items, works if the content renders itself to such a technique (e.g., seven habits of effective people, or Tony Robbins' RPM, Rapid Planning Method). Sometimes people stretch their ideas to fit into a category: "I will share the three K's of communication: Katch 'em, Keep 'em, Konvince 'em." Or for setting goals, the acronym GOALS: Gestation, Observation, Activation, Legislation, Stimulation. Yuck.

To be able to explain things easily, develop solid visual thinking skills. Never speak about things that you cannot draw with a crayon. Pictures help focus listeners' attention quickly and can bring abstracts to life. Even the world of mathematicians was in a blur until Lorenz drew the "butterfly" picture of nonlinear dynamic systems (see *Complexity* section).

Visual thinking skills are critical when you explain complex concepts. To develop them, learn how to look for patterns in complex elements, such as a mountain or a forest. Study any element in nature that has irregularities and fractal qualities. The advantage of observing fractal qualities is that they are self-similar. If you look at the patterns of a flower or a branch, you will see them on other similar items. Also, as scientist Irene Sanderes observes, fractals are similar across scales: a rock is like a mountain. Hollywood knows how to take advantage of this, making magic out of such forms: a few cows become a herd, a few buildings become a massive city. Use the idea of fractals to notice shapes and patterns and relationships across your products and services. Draw them even if you do not have drawing skills. Become friends with the back of a napkin.

To train your eye, pay attention to details that you may miss: veins in a shoulder blade, a crack in the asphalt, a stamp on a letter. You may find unique visuals that are reminiscent of things you do, and therefore create vivid metaphors (e.g., "Looking at our company is like looking at a 19th-century stamp. The closer you get to it, the more you're fascinated by the details"). All such metaphors help to develop a deeper understanding of the issues that your business is experiencing.

To make things easy to understand, you can learn from the movie industry. Here are a few descriptions of movies taken from the online movie database, IMDB. Even though most movies have intricate plots and character development, notice the brief and clear introduction that they have.

> *Stepbrothers:* "Two spoiled guys become competitive stepbrothers after their single parents get hitched."

> *Vicky Christina Barcelona:* "Two girlfriends on a summer holiday in Spain become enamored with the same painter, unaware that his ex-wife, with whom he has a tempestuous relationship, is about to re-enter the picture."

> *Mirrors:* "An ex-cop and his family are the target of an evil force that is using mirrors as a gateway into their home."

Notice the brevity of the statements. Too often a 30-second introduction gets diluted by presenting it in 3 minutes. Stay succinct. Imagine if your introductions could offer such an easy entrance to your topic as Hollywood movies do. The trick is to avoid making it too easy. If the topic is too easy to understand, people get bored. If it's too difficult, they get confused. You have to get it just right, almost like cooking a soufflé.

To deliver clear content, avoid convoluted phrases and jargon: "Integrating four-high performance synergistic processing engines (SPEs) and hardware dedicated to decoding and encoding of MPEG-2 and H.264 video, enables this processor to realize an optimized balance of processing flexibility and low power consumption." Better to say "This hardware helps you edit video without slowing you down."

The ability to turn complex things into clear things is a skill of the future. Do not be surprised if one of the job titles that will soon appear in an HR catalog is **Clarity Expert** – a person required to decode and scale back complex systems so we can understand them. Start practicing.

indulgence

Too many presenters speak too much about themselves. Have you heard presentations that start like this?

> "Hello everyone, my name is Jim, I am so happy to be here. Thank you so much for inviting me. I have been an environmental engineer for ten years. I work for one of the world's most influential environmental firms and have undertaken three prestigious energy efficiency projects in the past year. My company has 235 locations worldwide and I cater to a global customer…"

Can you imagine if the conductor first introduced himself and started talking about his accomplishments before the first piece of the symphony? There is way too much preoccupation with self. "Energy costs are keeping you up at night, and here are three ways you can avoid that…" is a much better, more attention-grabbing alternative to the introduction above because it focuses immediately on the listener. Save personal accomplishments for later in the presentation, if you feel they add credibility and are important to share. If you have the luxury of someone introducing you, ask that person to share details about you instead.

Presentations should not be narcissistic exhibitions. Presenters who look at them as an opportunity to broadcast themselves are better off choosing Facebook instead. Besides, looking inside can become dull even for the most beautiful and accomplished presenters; looking outside can keep you more interested and curious.

Imagine that this was a presentation about how to handle email better.

> "Suppose you need to reach me with an urgent email? Try hitting Send at precisely 10:47. Statistically speaking, that's when my most crucial messages arrive each day – and when I'm most likely to ping you back. How do I know this? Because I've been using a new software app called..."

Do you notice the focus on the speaker? How about if we switched the angle?

> "What time do you receive most of your crucial email messages? [Pause, acknowledge audience replies.] Would you find it helpful if you knew with statistical precision when your most important messages are likely to arrive? [Pause, the answer is likely yes.] Why would it be important to you? [repeat a few replies from the audience] You're absolutely right. The purpose of today's presentation is to introduce you to a new software and show you how to use it to manage your inbox better and save time."

Speaking is an act of giving, an act of generosity. Address the audience to serve them. For good examples on giving to the audience right away, look at popular magazines such as *Better Homes and Gardens*, *Reader's Digest*, or a health magazine (see article titles below). Editors know the secret of large circulation: readers are selfish.

> "Simplify Your Day"
> "How to Boost Your Brain Power"
> "What your eyes reveal about what's in your mind"

Picture your audience with remote controls in their hands. They can shut you off at any point.

There *are* times when you can get away with speaking about yourself in the first 30 seconds:

Self-deprecation. "My name is Tucker Max, and I am an asshole. I get excessively drunk at inappropriate times, disregard social norms, […] and just generally act like a raging dickhead. But, I do contribute to humanity in one very important way: I share my adventures with the world." (Tucker Max, famous writer) Or… "I know you want to hear the latest dope from Washington. Well—here I am." (Senator Alan Simpson)

Major drama. "In the morning of the stroke, I could not walk, talk, read, write, or recall any of my life. I essentially became an infant in a woman's body." (Jill Bolte Taylor, brain scientist)

Your last speech or lecture.

Unusual goal: "Hi, my name is Sarah Palin and I am going to sell a luxury jet on eBay." (Sarah Palin attempted this when she became governor of Alaska and removed unnecessary items from the office.)

Notable job function. "Hi, my name is Karen, and I am a rocket scientist. I work for NASA as a flight director and I am here to tell you about…" (I actually attended the presentation and it was annoyingly cool to witness her introduction.)

If you wonder what topics get attention right away, use any of the ones below. Tie any of these to your topic and you're bound to deliver an altruistic beginning.

Advancement (professional, financial, or social)	Improved appearance
Comfort	Leisure
Competence	Money
Efficiency	Personal prestige
Enjoyment	Security in old age
Freedom from worry	Self-confidence
Health	Time

To get attention, speak to people's aspirations. Or to what annoys them. You can address things that you know bug them (e.g., corporations saying "We care about you," people listening to mp3 players unaware of their surroundings, barefoot travelers at airport security lines, waiters who introduce themselves and speak like robots, or shrinking leisure time). Provide ways for them to cope.

As you focus on the listener, go beyond the overly hyped chicken soup for the soul, or "the secret." Find out your audience's "secret pain" or aspiration and deliver your own truth.

Don't stare into your reflection for too long. Instead of thinking *me*, *my* agenda, all *my* details, and *my* important tone, think *they*, what *they* want to hear, with few details, and in a friendly, personal, chatty way. No need to talk about your accomplishments that much. Most participants will have Googled you before you showed up anyway.

staging

Why is staging so important in presentations? If there is such a thing as the power of the mind, there is also such a thing as the power of place. Just think of how you respond to the environment through your circadian rhythms and how you stay alert during the day and conserve energy at night. Think what happens to your mood and behavior when you do not get enough exposure to daylight. Think of how you feel in a recently cleaned room. Surroundings can influence thoughts, emotions, and actions.

If you can create an environment where the audience anticipates your presence, your beginning (and the rest of the speech) is likely to be more powerful. You may not have access to light designers, sound engineers, decorators, drummers, or a flying tram (used in the opening of the Melbourne Commonwealth Games). But there are low-scale versions of event design. If you have a clear objective and a theme to go with it, you can use elements such as space, sounds, colors, and visuals to set up an atmosphere that has emotional appeal, creates curiosity, and provides various sensory experiences.

The easiest element to play with is **space**. Regardless of your budget, prompt yourself to think of creative ways to use space to design a framework for your event, set boundaries, or create vast areas. Then you can fill up the space with decorative elements, lights, media, and sounds. Check out some examples on the next few pages.

Would you rather attend a presentation in a room that looks like this?...

Or in a room that looks like this?...

Staging can also be done by using **props**, which draw attention (the focus is away from the presenter), reinforce an idea, and may even invite some humorous interaction. You can use chairs, posters, looping slide shows, memorabilia, or other objects related to your topic (minus rubber chickens). When Jill Bolte Taylor, brain scientist, delivers a speech on brain functions, she usually brings a real brain in front of a non-scientific audience. Imagine the first 30 seconds of her speech, as she introduces the left and right hemispheres, showing a dissected brain. Another presenter starts speeches on abundant cell phone use by showing a shoe stabbed with a knife and telling the story of a person who refused to shut her cell phone at the movies and got in trouble.

Creative use of chairs can set up an intriguing stage (consider the example of a teacher who removes all the chairs the first day of class and asks the puzzled students "what it would take to earn a chair"). Other presenters rearrange chairs to create a conversational space, or remove chairs from the back to invite participants to sit up front, or even block the entrance with chairs to observe what participants do and comment on their efforts to enter in the beginning of the speech. In a presentation I attended, the speaker started by saying "Please look underneath your seats. One of you has a $100 bill taped to it." Imagine the excitement. Such a fun use of props gives you opportunity for continuous wit: "Now you know that in order to make a buck, you have to get off your butt. Today, we will discuss the new strategy for penetrating European markets…"

Color is a useful tool in staging. You can be playful with the color of the furniture, or use colorful light bulbs for unusual light effects, or distribute colored paper as handouts… Your message will dictate whether to pacify users with tranquil earth tones or trigger strong emotions with a pulsing neon. Use color as an attention-getter, both inside and outside the presentation room, and as part of your "show." Some presenters start with a colorful projected graphic to draw attention.

In rooms where you routinely give presentations, can you paint walls and ceilings with fun colors? Can you move from an institutional white color to a pleasant light gray? Can you create a floor that reflects light, or modern countertops for the desks? Can you have tables with glass tops, which don't take that much visual space, especially if you present in small rooms? Who says you can't liberate some pieces of furniture from their designated function and bring them to the conference room? I know someone who is using nicely decorated kitchen cabinets in the boardroom. Another uses plastic shrimp-cocktail plates and clear shower rings to create Art Deco-style chandeliers.

Budget permitting, hire an interior decorator for the rooms where you typically present. Interior decorators know how to use space, color, and light to create a decor that tells a story. They have an eye for using even ordinary objects with style and modern simplicity (buffets, chalk boards, napkins, lamps, books, plants, photos in simple frames with neutral tones, salvaged cogs, or desks that defy workplace conventions). Reading these examples, can you think of one thing you could change about the room where you present?

Staging can give the impression that the event is unique—it may not be repeated the same way again. This creates excitement, or what Emil Durkheim, the French sociologist, called "collective effervescence," where everyone has a chance to feel the intensity of sensory stimulation and enjoys belonging to the group and the experience.

ALIENATED

Images can be useful staging tools, especially when they paint pictures we otherwise could not see. When was the last time you saw a picture that had to do with an inner image, something reflecting matters of the heart? The typical images used during a presentation focus on the external. Challenge yourself to stage an event with images that denote matters of the soul.

In a recent presentation, a manager used the image below as a giant poster that participants could see when they entered the room. The purpose of the talk was to motivate the audience to stop imitating the past and following old scripts. She created the image because in her department, everyone believed that you had to capitalize all letters in a title. The poster was meant to stage the beginning of the speech by proving that people read scanning the top of the words, and capital letters hindered legibility. Capitalization was a thing of the past. And so were a few of the team's work processes.

A taxi is a vehicle that disappears when it rains

Whether you display visuals electronically, clip them to the wall, or show actual objects, you can use them in the first 30 seconds to stage your speech, promote thinking, help the audience understand complex issues, or create curiosity and build anticipation for the rest of the session.

Humans are shaped by the environment.

Lights, colors, graphics, sounds…

Don't just schedule a presentation.

Stage it.

Speak to stand out

Good beginnings, bad beginnings

An author I know recently published a book and presented it to an audience in Romania. He started his book signing speech this way: "A book is like a parachute. You have to open it to appreciate it." This may seem like a good attention getter (much better than "Hi, I am Dr. X and so honored to be here"). However, a parachute in Romanian is also a derogatory term used to denote a lady of easy virtue. Ouch. It would have been safer to test that line with a few listeners prior to the speech.

Here is another example of a bad start: "I had a terrible day. This morning my collar button fell off. On my way here, the handle of my briefcase fell off. You know, I'm afraid to go to the men's room!" This joke has been so overly used as a speech starter that it's almost become a cliché.

How can you be off to a bad start? Untested lines, overly used and poorly delivered humor, or quotes by famous leaders (if I don't ever hear a Churchill quote at the beginning of a speech, it will be too soon). Another stale technique is the typical dictionary definition used in the introduction: "Webster's defines leadership as …" or the cinemascope introduction, with the typical phrase "Throughout history, one thing has been true…"

After a poor beginning, it will take you at least 10 minutes to recover.

Storytelling

Stories generate emotions. People like to feel, to be scared, even to sense conflict. Facts may inform and illuminate but it's stories that make your content more memorable. In fact, stories are not only what we remember, but *how* we remember. Even the *Harvard Business Review* uses stories (in the form of case studies) to attract its readers and help them feel and see the content better.

Take any chance to turn your content into stories. If you're concerned that you do not have any stories to share, just study your environment. Virginia Woolf, famous author, claimed that what we experience in a day contains almost everything we need to know about life. You can also extract stories from magazines that your audience is likely to read (*New York Times*, *Wall Street Journal*, *Forbes*, *Fortune*). This will help you relate your topic to current events.

If you create your own stories, read more on how to design one with well-defined characters, good flow, and emotional epic. Carol Shields, a Pulitzer Prize-winning novelist, described how to add texture and ignite interest with her stories: "I wanted wallpaper in my novels, cereal bowls, cupboards, cousins, buses, local elections, head colds, cramps, newspapers…"

Practice your stories so you can bring your own epic to life with a bit of rhythm and a lot of soul. Don't rely too much on improvising stories, especially in the first 30 seconds. Also, don't start by saying "Let me tell you a story."

Break traditions

Break traditions

The presentations that you still remember today are probably the kinds where presenters took some risks and had some edge. When you deliver your own, move away from conventional thought. Dare to say what no one has said before but has always thought. Better to create a little uneasiness than contentment. Audacious beginnings are interesting beginnings:

"It sucks to be one of the two birds killed with one stone."

"Who has a clue when to use a semicolon?"

"Are men funnier than women?"

"Nipple is a funny word."

Have a bold disregard for norms and allow your imagination to have fun. In a recent acting class I learned to keep asking "What if?" As Mel Helitzer comically puts it, "What if you actually saw McNuggets on a chicken? What if alphabet soup consistently spelled out obscene words? What if the leaning tower of Pisa had a clock? After all, what good is the inclination if you do not have the time?"

Constantly find taboos and break them. Tom Peters used to say that one of his nightmares was for his tombstone to read "He made budget." Become known for things other than compliance. Go for what is counterintuitive or challenges authority. Oh, one reminder: some intros are clever only the first time. Stay on the lookout for new ones.

Sustain attention

A strong beginning is enhanced by a strong follow-through. This is where concepts such as content organization, visuals, words, vocal power, varied presentation approach, and body gestures are very important.

Work on mastering the means of your expressions first. Know that all inner experiences have an outer physical expression. All that we feel inside—desires, ambitions—is somehow expressed through physical actions; the movement of the head, shoulders, spine ...they express something even before we are aware of it. Can you modulate your voice so it is varied and almost singsongy? Can your body speak when there are no words? Sincerity is not only expressed through words but also through gestures, glances, silences. Each motion of the body, even if you speak virtually, should be the expression of your soul.

An effective way to sustain attention is to pick a recurring "theme" and repeat it throughout the presentation. Obama's inauguration speech included a convincing "yes, we can," as an attention-sustaining and participatory mantra.

Each time you go out to present, make it be as if it were the first time. If you simply repeat the motions from other similar events, the presentation stops being alive. Each presentation, even though it may have the same content, should be different. And don't feel like you have to be an entertainer; in fact, research shows that activities driven by interest tend to last longer than activities driven by enjoyment.

Breathe life into the presentation, make it alive, tangible, exciting. Don't start unless you do it with the utmost passion.

Start with the end

Author Tod Goldberg confesses how he gets started: "A word, or an image, or an emotion will come to me, along with a person who feels it, and then a world sort of develops in my mind: Who would feel this? Why would they feel it? Next thing I know, I've got a big mug-o'-coffee, sad music on the stereo, I'm dressed in all black and typing." I wish speakers only showed up in front of an audience when they have a strong emotion or image to share. Too often, prior to a presentation, speakers sit in front of PowerPoint, pouring thoughts into bulleted text, without wondering "Who would feel this?" and "Why would they feel it?" A beginning is a promise to your audience, both emotional and intellectual. Reflect on what you would like them to be able to feel or do or think as a result of your presentation and base your beginning on those emotions.

Tod and lots of other authors agree that by the time they reach the end of their novels, they will return to the beginning for final touches. It's typical for authors to re-write the introduction multiple times once they have inked the ending.

When you start with a strong beginning (which is crystallized in the ending), you increase your chances to deliver ideas that people can act on; you will get the parted lips and widened eyes; you will convince them to show up to hear you again and again. And one final measure for an outstanding beginning. Write it down. Look at it. Is this something that your audience would want to clip on their refrigerators?